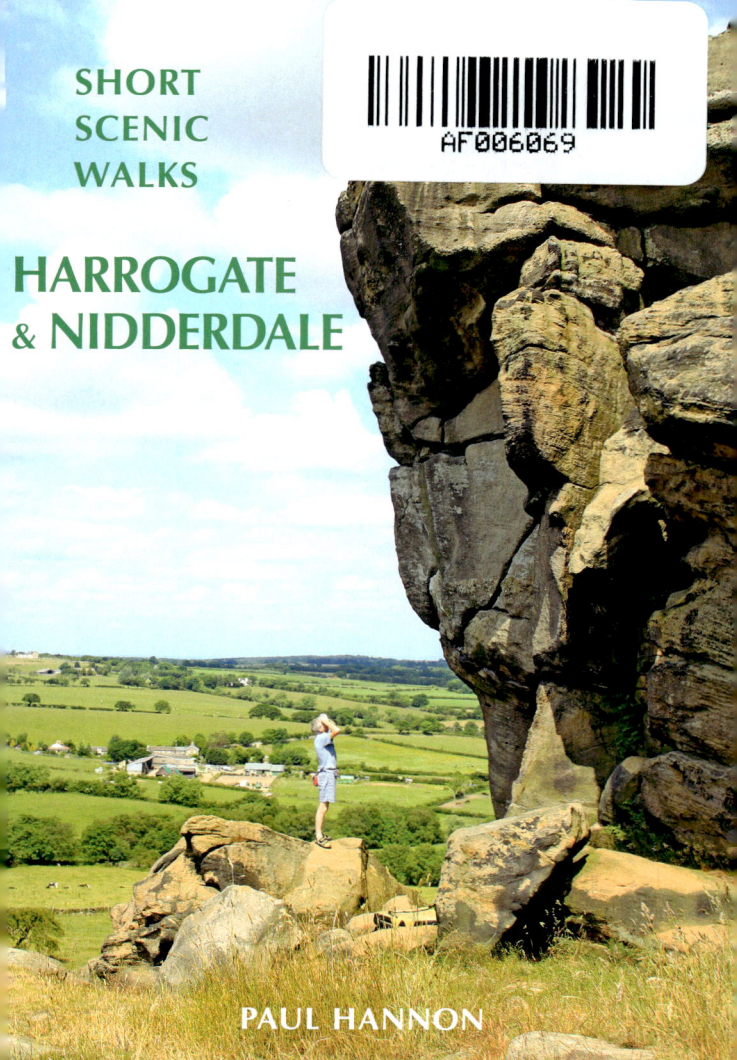

SHORT SCENIC WALKS

HARROGATE
& NIDDERDALE

PAUL HANNON

HILLSIDE PUBLICATIONS
2 New School Lane, Cullingworth, Bradford BD13 5DA

First Published 2019 © Paul Hannon 2019

ISBN 978 1 907626 29 6

While the author has walked and researched all these routes for the purposes of this guide, no responsibility can be accepted for any unforeseen circumstances encountered whilst following them

Sketch maps based on OS 1947 1-inch maps

Cover illustrations: Brimham Rocks; Washburn Valley
Back cover: Knaresborough Page 1: Almscliff Crag
(Paul Hannon/Yorkshire Photo Library)

Printed in China on behalf of Latitude Press

HILLSIDE GUIDES... cover much of Northern England

- 50 Yorkshire Walks For All
- Journey of the Wharfe (photobook)

Short Scenic Walks
- North York Moors
- Harrogate & Nidderdale
- Upper Wensleydale
- Lower Wensleydale
- Swaledale
- Malhamdale
- Sedbergh/Dentdale
- Ingleton/Western Dales
- Ilkley
- Aire Valley
- Haworth
- Hebden Bridge
- Bowland
- Around Pendle
- Ribble Valley

Walking in Yorkshire
- North York Moors South & West
- Nidderdale & Ripon
- Wharfedale & Malham
- Aire Valley & Bronte Country
- Yorkshire Wolds
- South Yorkshire
- North York Moors North & East
- Three Peaks & Howgill Fells
- Wensleydale & Swaledale
- Harrogate & Ilkley
- Howardian Hills & Vale of York
- Calderdale & South Pennines

Lancashire/North West/North Pennines
- Bowland
- Pendle & the Ribble
- Arnside & Silverdale
- Lunesdale
- Eden Valley
- Alston & Allendale

Visit us at www.hillsidepublications.co.uk

CONTENTS

Introduction..........................4

1 Thruscross Reservoir........6
2 River Washburn.............. 8
3 Timble Landscapes.........10
4 Fewston Reservoir.......... 12
5 John o'Gaunt's Castle....14
6 Dobpark Bridge............. 16
7 Farnley & Lindley...........18
8 Almscliff Crag................ 20
9 Kirkby Overblow............22
10 Spofforth Pinnacles........ 24
11 Around Follifoot.............26
12 Knaresborough...............28
13 Nidd Gorge....................30
14 Harlow Carr................... 32
15 Hollybank & Clint..........34
16 Above Birstwith.............36
17 Nidd Valley.................... 38
18 Braisty Woods................ 40
19 Brimham Moor..............42
20 Panorama Walk..............44
21 Tramway to Wath.......... 46
22 Foster Beck Watermill... 48
23 Guise Cliff......................50
24 Greenhow Mines........... 52
25 How Stean Gorge.......... 54
26 Thrope Edge.................. 56
27 Scar House Reservoir.... 58
28 Eavestone Lake..............60
29 Studley Royal................ 62
30 The Ure at Ripon...........64

Lindley Wood   *Yorke's Folly*

3

INTRODUCTION

In the heart of Yorkshire, Harrogate and Nidderdale combine to form a superb walking area where the Pennine moors roll down to the Vale of York. The western half is based upon the River Nidd and its neighbour the Washburn, an upland region of the Yorkshire Dales set within the Nidderdale Area of Outstanding Natural Beauty. To the east, the floral town of Harrogate and its colourful partner Knaresborough are major tourist attractions, as is the tiny cathedral city of Ripon. One of the brightest jewels in the Yorkshire crown is Fountains Abbey & Studley Royal, with impressive ruins and a beautiful setting. The rolling countryside surrounding Harrogate offers delightful country walking amid stone villages such as Follifoot and Kirkby Overblow, with natural landmarks such as Almscliff Crag and Norman castles at Knaresborough and Spofforth.

Nidderdale is probably least known of the major valleys of the Yorkshire Dales: above Pateley Bridge it is a well-defined upper Dales valley, increasingly steep flanks rising above the narrow dale floor to moorland heights. Sleepy little villages such as Middlesmoor and Lofthouse straggle out towards reservoirs that occupy a bleak setting, and both these villages look down on the fascinating ravine of How Stean Gorge. Downstream from Pateley Bridge the Nidd Valley is far more pastoral, sweeping gracefully through a landscape of fields and woodland to terminate at Ripley. This gateway village boasts a unique character, while neighbours Hampsthwaite, Birstwith and Dacre Banks are all a delight. Even below Pateley Bridge there remain glorious pockets of moorland, most famously at Brimham Rocks and Guise Cliff.

The unassuming Washburn Valley flows into the River Wharfe on the edge of Otley, and has long been a firm favourite of local ramblers. Its winding miles see a chain of reservoirs harness the River Washburn in a manner that has largely blended in well, cushioned as they are by richly wooded slopes. The valley is also rich in birdlife and has numerous historic features.

Whilst the route description should be sufficient to guide you around, a map is recommended for greater information and extra interest: Ordnance Survey Explorer maps OL289, OL297, OL298 cover all but two walks, which are found on OL30 and OL299.

HARROGATE & NIDDERDALE
30 Short Scenic Walks

27 Scar House

25 **26** Lofthouse

30 **Ripon**
29
Sawley **28** Fountains Abbey

Pateley Bridge **20**
24 **21** **22**
Greenhow
23
Bewerley **19** Brimham Rocks
Dacre Ripley
18 Banks **15**
Thruscross Birstwith **17** **Knaresborough**
1 **16** **13** **12**
Blubberhouses **2** Hampsthwaite Bilton
Swinsty **Harrogate** **14**
5
4 Follifoot **11**
Timble **3** Fewston
10
Norwood Bottom **6** Huby **9** Spofforth
8 Kirkby Overblow
Leathley **7**

- Nidderdale AONB, The Old Workhouse, King Street, Pateley Bridge HG3 5LE (01423-712950)   *www.nidderdaleaonb.org.uk*
Tourist Information
  - Royal Baths, Crescent Road, Harrogate (01423-537300)
  - Station Square, King Street, Pateley Bridge (01423-714953)
- Castle Courtyard, Market Place, Knaresborough (01423-866886)
  - Town Hall, Market Place, Ripon (01765-604625)

1. THRUSCROSS RESERVOIR

4½ miles from Thruscross

A reservoir circuit with a splendid moorland sandwich

Start Yorkshire Water's Thruscross Reservoir car park on Reservoir Road at west edge of dam (SE 153573; HG3 4BB)
Map OS Explorer 297, Lower Wharfedale & Washburn Valley

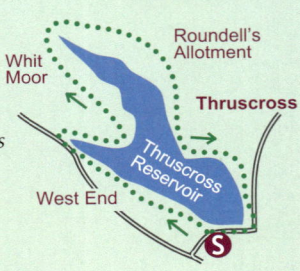

Thruscross Reservoir is the highest and youngest of the four Washburn Valley lakes, its 120ft high dam constructed in 1966. Sacrificed was the hamlet of West End, which has returned to view in times of drought - notably in 2018. A mile north of the start is the isolated Stone Cross Inn. Cross the road to a broad path down through Thruscross Woods to the reservoir. This runs an unbroken course along the bank, soon reaching the submerged West End-Thruscross road: trace it uphill a few strides to a footbridge to resume. Further, the reservoir's western arm passes a ruined mill. Its waterwheel socket is still evident, and beyond it you trace the course of the leat that supplied it. The feeder stream of Capelshaw Beck leads to a stile onto a road. Without joining it the path runs right to a footbridge, then up a verge to turn right through a gate. The path now traces the other side of this western arm beneath Whitmoor Farm, looking across at the mill before entering trees.

Part way along, just past the intriguing ruin of Holme Field Head in the adjacent field, you reach a stile on the left. Here leave the concession path and turn right outside the forest fence to a stile/gate onto Whit Moor. A path runs along the fenceside, and part way on merges with another at a guidepost to your left. This runs on to a stile by a gate to drop to a seat on the forest corner, overlooking the valley. A steep path outside the trees drops to a bridge on the River Washburn. This fine little beck draining the moors is currently unaware of what awaits it in the next few miles in the form of four large reservoirs!

Over a stile you stay in open country, beginning with a short climb to a bouldery knoll at the plantation corner. The path then rises more gently away across Roundell's Allotment. Beyond the plantations hiding the reservoir, moorland skylines lead from Rocking House to the Great Pock Stones. Intermittent marker posts see the path across the moor to pass beneath a small boulder cluster on a knoll. Over a stile/gate you enter heather moorland, a delightful section that ends all too soon. Back among bracken, and with the reservoir re-appearing, a broad grassy path drops right to a ladder-stile at the plantation corner. Steps drop you steeply by the trees to a path running left beneath sheep pastures above the lake.

Further on it drops to the shore, swinging left at a promontory where the dam appears ahead. After an inner corner it re-crosses the old road met earlier, and resumes along the shore until masked by trees. It continues parallel with a road until joining it: turn right past Thruscross Reservoir Lodge to the east end of the dam. Cross the dam road to finish, with steps at the end up into the car park.

Thruscross Reservoir

2   RIVER WASHBURN

3½ miles from Blubberhouses

Riverbank and fieldpaths amid unsung countryside

Start *Yorkshire Water's Blubberhouses car park (SE 168553; HG3 1SU), on A59 at head of Fewston Reservoir*
Map *OS Explorer 297, Lower Wharfedale & Washburn Valley*

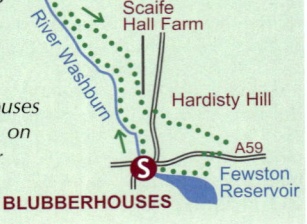

Blubberhouses is known largely for its location astride the busy Skipton to Harrogate road, though the Hopper Lane pub a half-mile up the steep climb towards Harrogate regularly waylays travellers. This scattered community also extends up Hardisty Hill featuring a smokehouse with cafe, while St Andrew's church sits south of the main road. It would have seen full congregations during construction of the reservoirs: Fewston's waters lap right up to the main road.

Cross the main road and just to the right a flight of steps descends to the River Washburn. An excellent permissive path heads upstream, remaining with the river for a considerable time. After the idyllically sited cricket club and a rocky scar on a bend you have open fields alongside. Across them is the distinct course of a tree-lined mill goit. Entering woodland the path runs alongside the extensive millpond of Low Dam to a path junction at a wall incorporating a seat. Although this is the walk's turning point, first continue beneath Limekiln Plantation to emerge into a clearing just prior to a ford/footbridge on the river. With a glimpse of the massive concrete dam of Thruscross Reservoir up-dale, the seat by the bridge makes a good place for a short break.

Back at the path junction by the stone seat, bear left on a path through a gate/stile, rising very slightly then on through scrub to a gate/stile into a field. A faint grass track crosses to a gate at the end. The firmer track runs on beneath a fence to arrive at Scaife

Hall Farm. From a gate on the left of the farm, steeply ascend the right side of a fence to a wall-stile onto Greenhow Hill Road at Hardisty Hill. Pause to enjoy a fine retrospective view over the farm to Kex Gill. Cross straight over and along an access road past a former Methodist chapel to a T-junction at scattered houses. Turn right to its early terminus at the last house. Big views look south over the head of Fewston Reservoir.

From a tiny gate in the corner take a gate in front to follow a walled grassy way, ending at a gate. Advance a little further with the wall, and at a gateway on a minor brow, take a stile on the right. Now follow the wall left along a field top, the wall crumbling as you steer a curious course around to the end, where you find a wall-stile above a streamlet. Advance the short way above the wooded streamlet to a wall-stile at a fence junction, and across the streamlet slant left up the field, being ushered right by an old boundary to a stile at a fence/wall junction. Here steps lead down onto a deep wooded hollow of the A59. Turn right on the verge and cross with care, quickly reaching a parking area. Here a stile by a gate sends a good path into Fewston Woods. Quickly forking, bear right down through a gateway onto the firm Fewston Reservoir path. Turn right on this around the head of the reservoir to rejoin the road just short of the car park.

Above Scaife Hall Farm

3   TIMBLE LANDSCAPES

3½ miles from Timble

The environs of Timble Gill offer rewarding surrounds between a lovely village and the River Washburn

Start Village centre (SE 179529; LS21 2NN), roadside parking
Map OS Explorer 297, Lower Wharfedale & Washburn Valley

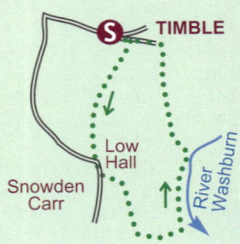

Timble is a tiny village on a broad ridge descending from the moors to the Washburn Valley, with the Timble Inn at its heart. From the phonebox take the byway left of the pub to join and go left on a back road. Leaving the houses, take a narrow enclosed footway on the right after Highfield Farm. This offers an unfailing descent to a confluence at Timble Gill Beck. Across, the path heads away within the confines of a tiny sidestream: ignore a gate on the right and the path rapidly escapes to run parallel. Before long the path runs left to a gate out into a field. Advance on with a fading old wall which points to an enclosed green way ahead. After a bend this resumes your course, running on above Holt Wood. From the left-hand of adjacent gateways a track continues along a field top to become enclosed, on above Manor House to join its drive. This leads out onto a narrow road at Low Hall.

Advance a short way beneath the open country of Snowden Carr, and 50 yards beyond Sandhill Farm's drive take a stile on the left. Swinsty Reservoir appears to the left, with Lindley Wood Reservoir down-dale. Slant right to a wall-stile and maintain the slant to a ladder-stile above Carr Farm. Cross the drive and on to a corner stile, and on the next field bottom to a stone slab and stile. Rising above trees ahead is the ruin of Dobpark Lodge, a 17th century hunting lodge. Cross to a gateway onto an old green way, and from a stile/gate opposite an enclosed way runs on to bridge Snowden Beck, then rises to a grassy fork beneath Midge

Hall Farm. Take the left branch which runs to a small gate into Dobpark Wood, and the path descends near its left edge.

Ignoring any branches, towards the bottom it forks: take the right branch over a streamlet to run on to a wall at the wood edge above Snowden Beck's steeper confines. Through a couple of stiles you emerge into a lower section of woodland with sensational springtime bluebells. The path drops down to a gateway in the bottom corner, and forks. Go left, dropping to a small gate by Snowden Beck. Go right a few yards then cross it, the path bearing right through trees to a gateway alongside the River Washburn. Follow this pleasantly upstream through a couple of sheep pastures: in the third a path forms to scale a small bank, slanting back down to a footbridge on Timble Gill Beck.

Across, turn left with the gill, an old wall coming in before you rise to a gateway to be deflected above the steep wooded bank. Climbing outside the trees, when it drops away a delightful bank top leads to a stile in a tiny section of wall, then along a fenceside to a gate just beyond. Don't pass through but turn up the wallside. From the top corner stile, cross a tiny area of tree plantings to a ladder-stile then resume up the wallside. A stile at the top admits onto a walled cart track. Go left, becoming surfaced at Book End Farm to absorb the outward route.

In Dobpark Wood

4 FEWSTON RESERVOIR

3³⁄4 miles from Fewston

Leisurely lakeshore strolling on firm pathways

Start Yorkshire Water's Swinsty Moor car park above Fewston dam (SE 186537; LS21 2NP)
Map OS Explorer 297, Lower Wharfedale & Washburn Valley

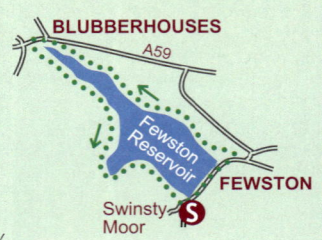

Swinsty Moor car park is a popular starting point for walks around both Swinsty and Fewston reservoirs, and also features WCs, a fishing office, and often an ice cream van. Nearby, across the dam just off-route, is Fewston church. It is difficult now to imagine Fewston as the community it was before the reservoirs came: a tiny Post office survived into the 1990s. From the car park rejoin the road and turn right to cross the embankment on a roadside footway. Most of the reservoir is on view here, largely surrounded by trees as is the glimpse of Swinsty Reservoir downstream. Both were constructed in the 1870s, each covering 153 acres and holding 850 million gallons.

At the far end ascend a stepped path into trees on the left just beyond Fewston Cottage (the old keeper's house). Turn left on a path at the top - not as per map, despite having been like this for many years. The broad path runs a short way through trees before a gentle drop to the shore. This earns a massive open view, its wilder feel enhanced by a moorland skyline high above sheep pastures on the other bank. This firm path leads unfailingly all the way along the northern shore beneath dense plantations. Towards the head of the lake the path curves around beneath the now parallel A59 - again not as per map, but in existence for many years. The path emerges onto a roadside footway to turn the two minutes left over the River Washburn to reach Blubberhouses car park.

Blubberhouses is known largely for its location astride the busy Skipton to Harrogate road, though the Hopper Lane pub a half-mile up the steep climb towards Harrogate regularly waylays travellers. This scattered community also extends up Hardisty Hill featuring a smokehouse with cafe, while St Andrew's church sits south of the main road. It would have seen full congregations during construction of the reservoirs: Fewston's waters lap right up to the main road.

The return path begins at the end of the car park. This is largely a pleasanter walk, the first stage offering more open views both over the reservoir, and over the pastures on your right. A sizeable arm on this side begins at a nice wooded knoll with little paths and seats. The path makes a loop around to bridge inflowing Thackray Beck, and soon returns to the main body of the lake. The last stage is a short one: with the dam approaching, a major fork at a little bay sees the right-hand path rise briefly through trees to emerge directly opposite the car park.

Fewston Reservoir

5   JOHN O'GAUNT'S CASTLE

4¼ miles from Swinsty

Varied surroundings as reservoirs of two valleys are linked

Start *Yorkshire Water's Stack Point car park (SE 198537; HG3 1SX)*
Map *OS Explorer 297, Lower Wharfedale & Washburn Valley*

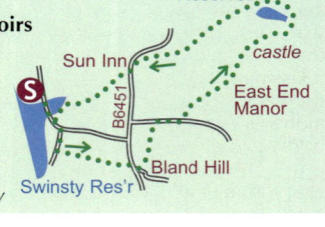

Rejoin the road and turn right over Swinsty Lagoon embankment. After the road swings away from the reservoir, fork right at the end of the trees. On a slight brow take a gate/stile on the left to ascend a walled green way. Through a stile at the top ascend the wallside to a stile, then bear left to a stile along the top wall. Now follow a wall away to a stile onto the B6451 at Bland Hill. Cross to the footway and go right to a junction, then briefly left past Norwood Social Hall and left along a grassy drive between houses. This continues as an enclosed path to a stile into a field. Bear right up to a corner stile then along to the next corner: from a squeezer-stile trace the wall's other side to a gate/stile onto a road. Turn right as far as a stile on the left after two houses. A wallside path heads away to a stile, then follow the wall right to ascend a steep bank of concrete steps.

At the top go a few yards right to a gate into Brown Bank farmyard. Go right a couple of yards then left alongside farm buildings. Keep on past the house towards a second house. Don't enter but take a gate into the field in front, and head away with a wall on the left. Through a second field curve left to a corner stile, then bear right across two fields towards East End Manor. At its drive take a stile in front and cross the field outside its grounds. Through a gateway at the end drop left down a field with an old boundary on your left. John o'Gaunt's Reservoir appears below as you drop between a scant ruin and a line of trees to a fence-stile.

A grassy path rises right to a gate into Haverah Park Top. On your left are scant remains of John o'Gaunt's Castle, a 14th century hunting lodge. Through a gate at the end of the buildings slant left down a grassy way above a wall to the dam. Across, take a green track left outside the reservoir wall. This rises a little to resume above a grass bank to cross a streamlet. From a gate beyond, the way runs above a seat with a panorama over the lake. Resuming, the path bears left of a ruin to drop down a crumbling wallside to a kissing-gate. The path rises to meet a walled green way. Turn left on this to emerge onto the earthwork of Bank Slack, and go right along its length. At the end it narrows into a green way, through a bridle-gate and on to emerge beneath Bank End Farm.

The path slants left to a gate/stile, then crosses to a bridle-gate into a field. Cross to a gate ahead, then advance to a kissing-gate. Bear gently left across reedy pasture to an outer wall corner, and from the kissing-gate slant up a garden to the nearest house in a cluster. Turning right on the drive out, as it bends right take a gap in the wall ahead to the Sun Inn. Go left on the B6451 to the end of the car park, then turn down a short track opposite. Through a gate continue down the wallside to a gate/stile, then bear left down to a bridle-gate into trees. A good path heads away, later dropping between old walls to Swinsty Lagoon. Keep left to rejoin the road, and back over the embankment.

John o'Gaunt's Reservoir

6 DOBPARK BRIDGE

4 miles from Norwood Bottom

An iconic old bridge is the highlight of a walk featuring riverbank and green lanes

Start *Lindley Wood Viaduct on B6451 (SE 209499; LS21 2RA), roadside parking on north side*
Map *OS Explorer 297, Lower Wharfedale & Washburn Valley*

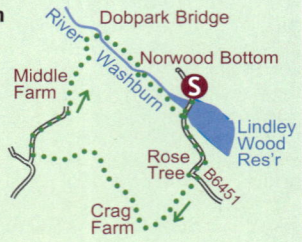

Cross the triple-arched viaduct and head away up the road, a prolonged rise above the reservoir swinging up to Rose Tree Farm. Fifty yards past it turn sharp right up the steeply climbing Crag Farm drive. When it swings right to the farm keep straight on the track above the buildings, now an enclosed cart track rising gently away beneath the wood to a gate out into a field. Simply remain on this improving track as the wood ends. It continues gently rising past a range of disintegrating walls before levelling out. Great views soon look over bracken slopes down into the valley, featuring Lindley Wood Reservoir.

Forge delightfully on until at the end the track turns left, through a gateway with a boundary stone inscribed 'F' at its base, and along through gorse to a moist corner with makeshift stepping-stones. From the corner gate a walled grassy way rises onto the cul-de-sac road to Dob Park. Turn right, descending with excellent views over the Washburn Valley. Further, the road winds down a steep wooded bank prior to its demise at Middle Farm. Note the old house with mullioned windows set back in the yard. A rough lane takes over to snake down to the valley floor, and brings arrival at Dobpark Bridge. This celebrated old bridge gracefully arches the wooded Washburn, matched by stone setts running down to a ford: it is the unofficial emblem of Washburn country.

Leave the old road climbing the bank, and from a stile on the right a path runs downstream through leafy Norwood Bottom, immediately joining a broader pathway. While not in intimate contact with the river, it affords good views over it to a wider landscape. After crossing an open meadow where the path follows the left-hand wall rather than the river, the way is taken across the river's tree-lined course on a water company bridge. The path resumes downstream to the head of Lindley Wood Reservoir, winding through verdant surrounds to a stile/gate back onto the B6451 at the end of the viaduct.

Opposite: River Washburn   *Dobpark Bridge*

7   FARNLEY & LINDLEY

4¼ miles from Leathley

Easy rambling linking two scattered old hamlets of the lower Washburn Valley

Start *Opposite church on B6161 (SE 232470; LS21 2JU), small parking area with honesty box*
Map *OS Explorer 297, Lower Wharfedale & Washburn Valley*

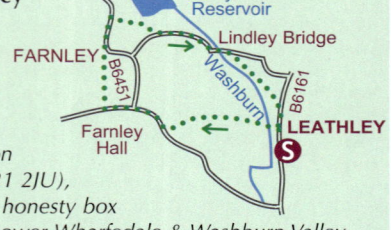

The scattered community of Leathley is centred on St Oswald's church, with its magnificent Norman tower and a nave from the same period, in the west doorway of which a Norman door is decorated with ironwork. Also on this brow are picturesque almshouses and old school of 1769. Turn north along the roadside footway, passing an old turnpike milestone. From a stile by a gate on the left just past it and a side junction, cross the field to a footbridge on the River Washburn. Turn right along the edge of this extensive arable field, your path briefly shadowing the river until woodland intervenes. Continue up the field outside a plantation, the path rising all the way to the field-top to a hedge-gap onto a road, where turn right.

Woodland opposite marks the grounds of Farnley Hall, a part Elizabethan house enlarged in the late 1780s. For centuries it was the seat of the Fawkes family, and Walter Fawkes was a patron of the artist Turner, a frequent visitor to the hall. At Home Farm, with its traditional courtyard incorporating a business park, a junction is reached alongside a lodge and a Queen Victoria memorial tap. The B6451 goes right while the hall drive goes left. Keep straight on, and a few minutes further, now with a proper footway, a stile set back in the hedge opposite gives access to park-like grounds. Follow the hedgerow away, undulating towards Farnley church. Surviving kerbstones confirm this as an old way from hall to church. At the end slant right up to a stile into the car park. The modest little All Saints church was rebuilt in 1851.

Joining the road go left, passing a farm to leave the hamlet's verges. As the road drops away escape through a gate set back on the right. Almost the full length of Lindley Wood Reservoir is revealed below, backed by a dense cloak of woodland. Follow the hedge on your right, gently declining through a gate/stile and continuing with a hedge down a longer field-top high above the dam wall. At the end a gate/stile put you onto a steep back road. Turn down this as it quickly swings right to run amid dense greenery to Lindley Bridge on the Washburn.

Across, take a gap on the right to descend a flight of stone steps. Heading downstream, a path squeezes between mill goit and fish farm, one restored to supply the other. Past the fishery drive the improved path resumes with the channel. Though drying up, its course is followed for some time through a stile and then a small gate out into a field, running beneath trees before dropping down to a bend of the river. Through a stile, head downstream on a potentially moist section of path. Things soon improve and the thinner path runs for a good while through unkempt grassland before crossing to meet the goit again at Mill House, the former Leathley Mill. Turn up its near side to follow an enclosed path out onto the B6161. The church is a short half-mile to the right, passing Leathley's exclusive properties as the verge-cum-footway leads back to the start.

Almshouses at Leathley

8 ALMSCLIFF CRAG

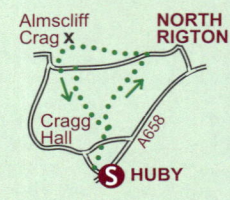

3½ miles from Huby

Easy walking to a celebrated rocky landmark and viewpoint

Start Crossroads by station
(SE 275475; LS17 0AJ),
roadside parking on Weeton Lane
Map OS Explorer 297, Lower Wharfedale & Washburn Valley

Huby is a scattered village with some nice corners. From the station cross the main road to Strait Lane. Follow it up towards the village edge, and look for paths signed both ways. Take the one on the right, a narrow snicket between houses to cross a low wall-stile to a fork in front of a field. Take the left branch, remaining enclosed behind gardens to Crossfield Cottage. Follow its drive up onto suburban Crag Lane. Cross to an enclosed path rising away, quickly swinging right to run along the backs of gardens into a field. This earns an impressive prospect of Almscliff Crag above. Advance on the field edge through a kissing-gate and continue to the far end. From a corner kissing-gate, drop through a wood corner to a streamlet and kissing-gate behind. A path slants up the field to a fenced wood above. Go briefly right then left with it to a kissing-gate onto a driveway serving Cragg Hall (Holly Hill on the map). From a stile opposite a path runs left around the field top to a stile into an old farmyard. Turn right on the track into a field.

Cross the field bottom to a stile in the hedge opposite, and on through a small scrubby field to a stile and streamlet. Now slant steeply left to a stile in a rising hedge, and maintain this line up across a number of fields, partly aided by white marker posts to a wall-stile onto North Rigton's Crag Lane. Turn briefly right to a seat on the left, enjoying a fine Wharfe Valley panorama. Minutes further is North Rigton, with its Square & Compass pub. Over the adjacent stile double back left, slanting up to a stile in the facing hedge. Across a drive head away with the wall on your right, drawn by close-at-hand Almscliff Crag. After two squeezer-stiles rejoin a right-hand wall running to a stile into the crag's environs. A path forms to rise to the rocks, which you can ascend to the crest of the major outcrop, High Man. Stop when you get here!

Almscliff Crag is a major Wharfe Valley landmark, and a popular venue for rock climbers. The extensive panorama includes the full girth of Rombalds Moor. A section of wall between the two main bluffs of High Man has a perilous stile in it to descend to the base of these main crags. Immediately below are further outcrops known as Low Man, with a path along their base. Go left here, above or below the crags, to some final boulders in a corner where an enclosed footway descends towards Cragg Farm.

A stile leads back onto Crag Lane, where turn left down to a small group of houses. After the last one (Cliff House) take a gate on the right, dropping to a stile by a gate just below. Slant across to a stile opposite, then turn down the hedgeside. From a stile in the bottom corner descend a field centre to a gate/stile in the hedge below, then down another hedgeside to a gate where a firm track forms. This descends outside a plantation to a gate into the grounds of Cragg Hall. Drop down to rejoin the outward route on the driveway and retrace your opening steps.

At Almscliff Crag

9   KIRKBY OVERBLOW

4 miles from Kirkby Overblow

Steady rambling with open views from around an attractive village

Start *Village centre (SE 325492; HG3 1HD), roadside parking*
Map *OS Explorer 289, Leeds* **or** *297, Lower Wharfedale & Washburn Valley*

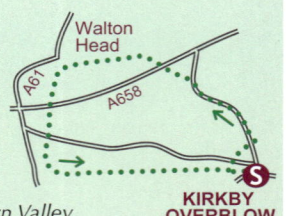

Kirkby Overblow sits clustered on an exposed hilltop ridge between the Wharfe and the Nidd. From the Shoulder of Mutton cross to a lane on the top side of the Star & Garter. Keep on into the churchyard, passing All Saints church with its 15th century tower to a stile at the far end. Cross a lawn to a stile onto a drive, then bear right onto a short enclosed path rising to a wall-stile into a field corner. Take the inviting enclosed path right, over a brow and down onto narrow Walton Head Lane. Go briefly right then take an enclosed path on the left. This descends a delightful course to emerge onto a road opposite Brig Hall, former almshouses. Turn left up the broad verge and along the brow. Starting a gentle decline, leave by a stile on the left. Cross the field to a small gateway in the wall near the far corner, then on again to a fence-gate. Just behind is a stile onto the A658.

Cross with care to a stile in the hedge opposite, and cross the field to a gap in the hedge corner ahead. New views look over the Crimple Valley. Head away with the hedge on your right just as far as a gateway (not used), then turn sharp left and cross the field to a stile in the fence opposite, below a wood. Dropping away, merge with the right-hand hedge to approach houses at Walton Head Farm. Over a stile advance on the slim field outside the houses to a gate ahead, then bear left down the field to a stile and a footbridge in the fence. Head away with the hedge on your left, and from successive stiles at the end bear right to a hedge-stile onto the A658. With a wary eye on descending traffic in particular, cross to a stile opposite and escape along the field. This same course is maintained to approach a house (Crag View), not quite as per map: after a very brief enclosed section, keep the hedgeside to your right. The way bears left outside the garden wall, and on a short way to a stile into the grounds. Cross the garden to a stile onto the drive going left onto Walton Head Lane.

Cross to a stile and bear left over this small enclosure to a streamlet and stile, then ascend the fieldside rising away. By the time the brow is reached you have an excellent view south over the Wharfe Valley to Otley Chevin, while Almscliff Crag rises impressively above the fields around Huby. From a stile on the brow, descend the other side to a corner stile. Cross to another just to the left, then cross a couple of field tops of which the first is enclosed above a horse paddock: new tree plantings are also encountered. From a stile at the end an open field is crossed to a bridle-gate, from where a hedgeside climb of a scrubby pasture leads to a kissing-gate atop the brow. Resume above the hedge on your right, pleasantly on two lengthy fieldsides above a wooded bank. At the end the church tower is revealed ahead. At the end of a couple of small fields you join the enclosed path from near the start. Pass through the wall-stile on the right to finish as you began.

Kirkby Overblow church

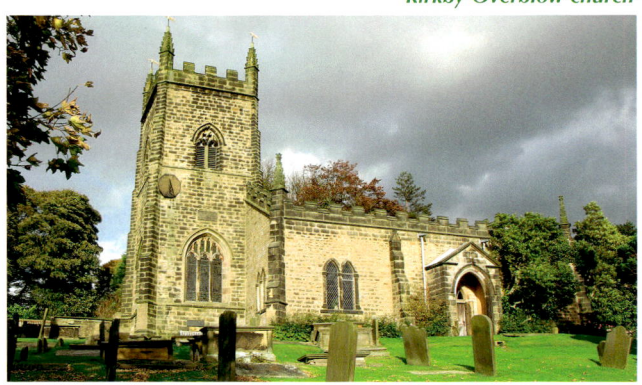

10   SPOFFORTH PINNACLES

4¼ miles from Spofforth

A beckside ramble leads to fascinating rock formations

Start *Village centre (SE 363510; HG3 1AP), roadside parking on Castle Street*
Map *OS Explorer 289, Leeds*

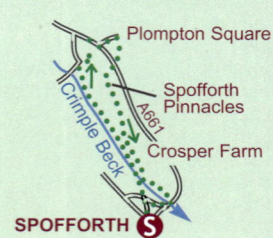

   Spofforth is an attractive village dominated by a ruinous 13th century castle. There are two pubs and a shop. All Saints church has a 15th century tower: John Metcalf, otherwise Blind Jack of Knaresborough, was buried here in 1810. Leave the road through the village by unsigned Church Lane opposite the shop. This runs past a triangular green and swings right past the church onto the A661. Go briefly left to cross Spofforth Bridge on Crimple Beck, then turn upstream on a path largely adhering to an embankment.
   Ignore a footbridge past the last building, and maintain this course all the way upstream to eventually reach Plompton Road at Guilders Bridge. Over to the right during this stage are massive outliers of Spofforth Pinnacles. Don't use the stile but turn right parallel with the road, and as it swings away maintain this line outside Brown Hill Wood up to a stile/gate onto the A661. Cross and follow the verge briefly right then turn left up a road to two lodges at Plompton. Off-route just past the lodges, a gate points the way to Plumpton Rocks. Open weekends and Bank holidays, March to October, a fee is payable to explore this 30-acre park boasting gritstone outcrops, woodland walks and an attractive lake.
   At the lodges turn right up the road to the houses at Plompton Square. Turn sharp right along the first row, continuing at the end on an enclosed path to a stile into a colourful pasture. Head away, bearing right to drop to a stile in the far corner. Re-cross the A661 to a stile, and a path heads away with a wall outside a wood to a gateway on a gentle brow. This overlooks the

Crimple Valley as you emerge into the environs of Spofforth Pinnacles. Bear gently left on a path dropping slightly but remaining near the area's left edge. You now look down on this fascinating collection of randomly sited gritstone monoliths amid bracken. The path runs to the nearest boulder then on beneath two further ones. Through a line of hawthorns an intermittent path continues to a fence corner outside a sprawling farm at Braham Hall. Through a stile you reach a wall corner at the far end of the confines.

Keep on to a minor knoll then descend the extensive field, bearing gently right to pass left of an outcrop and left of a marsh to a fence-stile. Bear right to follow the hedge on the bottom of the enclosure, passing a pond. Keep on through a gate and beneath further rocks amongst successive stiles beneath Crosper Farm. Emerging into a lengthy pasture, further boulders are evident nearby as you reach a fence-stile halfway along the hedge. Over this cross a slab bridge and bear left across the arable field to gain the embankment of the outward route. Turn left the short way to the footbridge, and this time cross it onto an enclosed path past the old cornmill. You also cross the dry channel of a former cut on a stone-arched bridge and out onto Mill Lane. At a junction at the top at the village edge, go a couple of steps left on Clive Road and then either keep left on Church Hill for the church, or sharp right on Beech Lane for the castle.

Spofforth Pinnacles

11   AROUND FOLLIFOOT

4 miles from Follifoot

Rambling by old railway, country lane and spacious parkland on the edge of a charming estate village

Start *Truncated section of Pannal Road alongside A658 junction west of village (SE 333524; HG3 1DR), roadside parking*
Map *OS Explorer 289, Leeds* **or** *Explorer 297, Lower Wharfedale & Washburn Valley*

    Advance to the side road's abrupt end at the last house, where an enclosed bridleway continues parallel with the main road. This drops to an underpass through which you shall return. For now advance straight on, rising slightly then swinging left to run a pleasant enclosed course to a sharp bend. Parallel on your left is the Church Fenton & Harrogate branch line, closed in 1964. When the bridleway goes right, pass through the kissing-gate in front and head away. A firm path remains underfoot, broadening into a cart track along the deep trench of the rail cutting. Go straight over an early cross-track and resume for some time between wooded banks.

    Reaching a minor clearing, leave by a firm path slanting left up to a kissing-gate, then double back left on an inviting fieldside path. Bear right at the end, briefly on a cart track, then left through a broad gap. The path descends the fieldside, swinging right at the bottom and becoming enclosed as it crosses Horse Pond Beck. Remain on this splendid hedgerowed way of Tofts Lane as it runs towards the village. At the head of a suburban street, remain on the track rising left past gardens before turning right to become a firm access lane at houses. Advance briefly on, then as it swings right take a wall-stile on the left. A tightly enclosed path runs right between gardens, twice swinging sharp left, then right at a junction to emerge onto the main street. Turn left to a T-junction in front of the imposing arch at Rudding Gates.

Follifoot is a little village of great character, with a Post office/shop and the Radcliffe Arms and Harewood Arms. From the green with its cross and stocks, turn right on Plompton Road to the church of St Joseph & St James. Your path takes a stile into the end of the churchyard, though first go a few steps further to view the circular pound which would have housed stray livestock. A stile at the churchyard bottom points down a hedgeside to a stile onto the A658. Cross with care to another stile and a short path drops onto a firm track. This tract of countryside is part of the Rudding Park estate, much of which is now a golf course. The present house dates from the 1820s, and operates as a hotel.

Go a couple of paces right then follow the track as it runs with a sturdy wall on your left, immediately onto the golf course. Remain with this wall all the way, turning sharp left at a cross-tracks, while further on at another track junction, a grassy path takes over. At the very end a fence-stile puts you onto a driveway at Rudding Dower. Turn right the short way out onto Rudding Lane. Turn left for a long, steady rise on broad verges outside Rudding Park. At the top it bends left to a junction just short of the A658. Turn right on Pannal Road, leaving at the first chance by a gate on the left sending an enclosed track down to the A658 underpass. Emerging to join the outward route, turn left to finish.

Harewood Arms, Follifoot

12 KNARESBOROUGH

4 miles from Knaresborough

Knaresborough's fascinating riverside features fill this easy and absorbing stroll

Start High Bridge (SE 345571; HG5 9AY), Conyngham Hall car park off A59 **Map** *OS Explorer 289, Leeds*

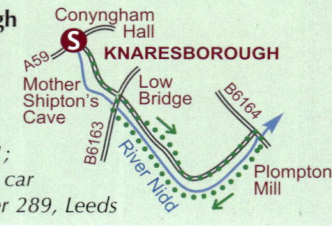

Knaresborough is a market town with bags of character, perched above a large bend of the Nidd. Overlooking the deep gorge are the ruins of Knaresborough Castle. Dating from the 12th century, it was extended by King John as a base for hunting in the old Forest of Knaresborough. What survives today is largely the 14th century work of Edward I and Edward II. An Elizabethan courthouse survives as a museum, and the castle grounds form a public park. At High Bridge is the entrance to Mother Shipton's Cave where you can discover the secrets of this 15th century prophetess, and witness countless articles turned to stone by waters from the Dropping Well. Your route takes the town side of the bridge, on the narrow road of Waterside past the Worlds End pub. Its colourful course passes under the rail viaduct and past boat landings and refreshments to reach Low Bridge.

Across the road resume on Abbey Road. Tall cliffs to your left feature the House in the Rocks, dating from 1791 and comprising four vertical rooms. Just past it is the Chapel in the Crag, a wayside shrine of 1408, its entrance guarded by a carved knight. Resume along the quiet road, soon between tall cliffs and the river. A traffic impasse is reached at splendid sandstone houses. Here a group of 13th century friars began work on a priory, thought to be on the site of a chapel that became St Robert's resting place. Further, the road reaches modern housing. A small gate on the right marks the entrance to St Robert's Cave, a few steps down into the trees, overlooking the river. A hermit for almost forty years until his death in 1218, his pilgrims included King John: the cave hewn from the cliff was his original chapel, with the base of its successor outside.

The road then joins the B6164 on the edge of town, where turn right over Grimbald Bridge then back upstream. An old drive runs to an open area between Plompton Mill Farm and Plompton Mill, now a café alongside a weir beneath a caravan site. Advance past the last of the caravans where a path squeezes up the wooded bank onto a splendid knoll beneath the sandstone Grimbald Crag. Here you look down on another weir supplying the former Abbey Mill on the opposite bank, with a waterwheel in place.

The path drops to the edge of the caravan site, but within a few steps bears right to run above the wooded bank. Dropping back to the river, it traces the Nidd through woodland. After passing a massive house opposite, you emerge into a field. The fenced path crosses it well above the river to reach a drive. Ignore its climb to the left, and keep straight on past a couple of houses, as a path squeezes beneath a massive limekiln. Back onto the riverbank the path resumes beneath steep woodland. A short pull towards the bank top precedes a drop back down to a garden wall, and on to emerge by an interesting house. Follow this lane past other houses out onto the B6163. Turn right past the Mother Shipton Inn and cross Low Bridge to rejoin your outward route.

Knaresborough Castle

13   NIDD GORGE

4½ miles from Bilton

First-rate wooded river scenery upstream of Knaresborough

Start *Old Bilton (SE 313576; HG1 4DH), car park on old railway on Bilton Lane, reached from A59 Skipton Road, Harrogate* **Map** *OS Explorer 289, Leeds* **or** *297, Lower Wharfedale & Washburn Valley*

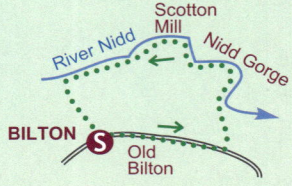

Modern housing at Bilton on the edge of Harrogate ends at the former railway that served Pateley Bridge, Ripon and points north. A plaque marks the course of a narrow-gauge mineral line that branched westwards from here between 1907 and 1956 to take coal to Harrogate Gasworks. Leave suburbia behind by heading away on the contrastingly quiet continuation of Bilton Lane. Almost at once on your left is the Gardeners Arms at Old Bilton. If it's open, then step inside to appreciate its old world charm.

Continue along the road, which swings up and around past a caravan site into more open surroundings. Passing through a gate followed by scattered dwellings, leave by a gate on the left at the end of a field after a small cluster of houses. An enclosed track runs the short way to a stile/gate into the woods of the Nidd Gorge, acquired by the Woodland Trust in 1995. The track runs left along the wood top, and when it passes through a locked gate take the broad path right, outside a fence on your left. Ultimately, at a fork, take the right branch slanting grandly down the partly open bank to the foot of the wood, with the River Nidd waiting below.

At the very bottom turn upstream past splendid surrounds with craggy walls opposite. This riverside path leads quite quickly to Burgess Bridge over the Nidd. Don't cross but resume on the path upstream, a splendid stroll by the river through Bilton Banks, with various sections reinforced by boards amid springtime bluebells. A brief spell well above its winding bank soon drops back down, with even a little spell by sandy beaches as you leave and then re-enter Woodland Trust land. Remaining hard by the riverbank, an open, scrubby section is met before a sustained spell almost draws level with Scotton Mill on the opposite bank.

Just before this point, an old way (the second of two within a minute) ascends from the riverbank, serving an old ford. Turn up its hollowed course, now with wooden steps, to a level path junction: bear briefly right to another junction just around the corner, and take the right branch slanting steadily back to the river at a weir. This served the former Scotton flax mill of 1798. Resume upstream just a short way further as far as a sidestream. From the main bridge take the path rising left away from the river, keeping right at a very early fork to emerge into a big field corner.

Take the path bearing right, following the wood edge to meet an old railway line alongside the Nidd Viaduct. Its 100ft tall arches were completed in 1848, carrying the old line to Ripon and points further north over the Nidd Gorge: it closed in 1967, and its parapet offers a good view of the river upstream. Turn left on the popular, surfaced path on the old line. Part way on are sculptures of two local characters and a 'Child of the Future'. This leads unfailingly back to the start.

Deep in the Nidd Gorge

14 HARLOW CARR

4¼ miles from Harrogate

Delightful gardens and woodland crags on the very edge of Harrogate

Start *Pump Room, Low Harrogate (SE 298553; HG1 2RY), car parks*
Map *OS Explorer 297, Lower Wharfedale & Washburn Valley*

The octagonal Royal Pump Room was at the heart of Victorian Harrogate's spa heyday, serving sulphur water to visitors. It has been preserved as a museum, and the brave can still sample its 'distinctive' taste. Cross the road into Valley Gardens and follow the streamside path to a cafe. This area is known as Bogs Field, where 36 of Harrogate's 88 mineral wells are found. Across the circular garden beyond the cafe, take the main path up the centre of the gardens: this soon reaches a wall corner on the right, just past the Magnesia Well Pump Room of 1858. The path resumes up the side of the gardens to ease out at a fork, with a war memorial set back to the right. Leaving tarmac, bear right on the inviting woodland path to the left of the cross. This runs pleasantly on through The Pinewoods to emerge onto Harlow Moor Road.

Directly opposite, a tarmac path rises gently back into woodland, soon reaching a large grassy clearing. Pass along its right side to head back into trees. The path soon emerges to run along the edge of the woodland, and passing Pinewood Farm it drops onto Crag Lane opposite Harlow Carr Gardens. Opened in 1950 to test the suitability of plants for the northern climate, the North of England's premier botanic gardens are run by the Royal Horticultural Society. The site was developed as a spa in the 1840s, when a bath-house and hotel were built and gardens laid out. Go right 100 yards and turn left down to the secluded former Harrogate Arms: this aforementioned hotel for the adjacent spa has been closed since 2013.

In the corner below, turn right through a small gate and a path sets off into trees outside the Harlow Carr fence, running a grand course above a stream. After bridging a streamlet you reach a path junction: take the right one slanting down to a footbridge. Going briefly downstream, the path quickly slants up the bank to pass through a fence gateway into more open woodland of birch, bracken and shrubs. Just yards further as the way splits, take the right-hand, ascending path, soon levelling out to meet the fence as a wall takes over. The path runs grandly on by the wall to quickly reach the edge of the gritstone buttresses of Birk Crag.

The path rises above the near side of the rocks, with their crest just to the left from where you can survey wooded Oakdale. Just to your right, the path climbs a few wooden steps to a path junction at a fence. Go right the few strides out onto an access road, and turn right on this into the open and on towards Harlow Carr again. Before the gardens however, take an enclosed path left opposite kennels. This rises to a gentle brow with open views, and maintains a firm course to emerge onto Cornwall Road at a mini-roundabout. Cross and follow Harlow Moor Road's footway right to the start of The Pinewoods. Ignore the first path left and advance a little further to where a path crosses the road. Go left on this through trees, its good, firm course returning to the memorial cross. Retrace steps through Valley Gardens, with variations as desired.

Harlow Carr Gardens

15   HOLLYBANK & CLINT

4 miles from Ripley

Easy rambling amid some historic features on the edge of a classic village

Start Village centre
(SE 284605; HG3 3AY),
car park   *Map* OS Explorer 298, Nidderdale

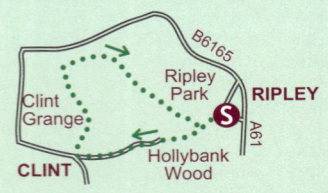

Ripley was a market town in 1357, and seat of the Ingilby family since before that. Nothing here is without interest, though the castle is the major attraction. First sight is the imposing early 15th century gatehouse. The castle was largely rebuilt in 1555 and was much enlarged in 1780. The lakes and deer park were laid out by Capability Brown and are open throughout the year. The castle is open at various times, daily in summer. Ripley also boasts the Boars Head pub, shops, farm museum and tearoom. This classic estate village was rebuilt by Sir William Amcotts Ingilby in 1827, based on a French village of Alsace Lorraine - note the town hall named the Hotel de Ville. The medieval market cross has stocks alongside. The church has 14th century effigies of Sir Thomas and Lady Ingilby. In the churchyard is a pre-Reformation weeping cross: the far from comfortably positioned sockets at the bottom cater for the knees of penitent souls.

From the square follow the side road between church and castle, becoming a surfaced pathway dropping down to cross Ripley Beck. Rising away outside the park wall, you have an early choice of paths. Look back for a glimpse of the castle above the lake. Until recently a pleasant bridle-path, this historic old way of Hollybank Lane is now graced with a tarmac surface for the benefit of cyclists. The track rises to meet a broader track at a corner of the park wall at Sadler Carr. In the trees in front is the site of a medieval manor house within a defensive moat. Keep left on the track ahead, running beneath fine oaks into Hollybank Wood.

Emerging at Holly Bank Lodge, advance along the narrow road, rising to meet a road in Clint at attractive Weavers Cottage. Your onward route takes a farm drive on the right, but first advance briefly straight on to see Clint Cross. Ancient stone tiers support a hollowed cross base, and old stocks stand alongside. The cross bears the inscription 'Palliser the Tailor', companion to an equally intriguing one at the start of Walk 16. Back on the farm drive this runs on to soon reach Clint Grange. After the first barn take a fence-stile on the left and resume parallel along the field edge. From a stile at the end slant left to a gate behind a track, and bear left up the large field to the left edge of a wood.

From the gate advance on outside the wood and around its far side to a corner stile. Across it head away from the wood with a fence on your left. After a couple of fields you approach the buildings at Whipley Hall. A bridle-gate on the left just before the corner sees you bridge a streamlet: resume along a paddock side outside the grounds to a corner bridle-gate onto the drive. Advance along this the short way to a surfaced fork, and bear right. This passes High Rails Farm to meet the estate wall again. Remain on this same way past the attractive Park Lodge, and the firm track shadows the park wall which contains a herd of fallow deer. This leads unfailingly back down to meet the outward route at Sadler Carr: turn left back into Ripley.

Ripley Castle

16 ABOVE BIRSTWITH

4¼ miles from Hampsthwaite

Beckside and riverbank walking on the southern slopes of the Nidd Valley

Start Village centre (SE 259587; HG3 2EU), roadside parking
Map OS Explorer 298, Nidderdale **or** 297, Lower Wharfedale & Washburn Valley

Hampsthwaite's focal point is an attractive green bearing a village pump: close by are the Joiners Arms, tearoom and shop, while a graceful old bridge spans the Nidd. From the green take the Birstwith road updale out of the village. After a few minutes you cross Bracken Bridge on Tang Beck: the intriguing inscription 'Palliser the Hatter' is a twin of the 'Tailor' on Clint Cross (Walk 15). Immediately over, take a stile on the left and head away upstream along this broad, shallow valley. A splendid section traces the beck tightly past Gormires Wood across it, through several fields to ultimately emerge onto a back road. Cross straight over to a wall-stile and resume. This time the valley takes some shape, and a thin path runs to a gap-stile ahead, just above the beck. Continue rising away to a bridle-gate in a hedge, then follow a hedge away to a corner gate. Here an enclosed grassy way runs on to join a drive outside Birstwith Hall, which leads out onto a road at a cottage and triangular green.

Turn right steadily uphill, and just beyond a junction leave the road where it bends right. A wall-stile in the corner sends you directly up the fieldside, rising to a ladder-stile in the very corner. Continue rising, passing through a fence-stile and rising to a wall-stile at the top corner onto another road. Turn right and down through a junction at Meg Gate, down past the entrance to a school at the former Swarcliffe Hall, and down into Birstwith. On the village edge you pass the elegant tall spire of St James' church.

At the bottom bear right to the village store junction, where go left past the school on the main street towards the River Nidd. Across the bridge is the Station Hotel. Before the river turn right towards the feed mill yard. The path diverts left of the mill, crossing the mill-race on a footbridge to shadow a perimeter fence around above the river. At the end double back right with the fence, along to a kissing-gate back onto the original line of the path. Here turn left on a wallside path outside trees, and from a kissing-gate at the end, drop down through a few trees to rejoin the riverbank. This leads pleasantly downstream, now for a considerable ramble. The point of leaving is at a bridle-gate back into a field, with a large barn up to the right. Slant up to it, where a kissing-gate puts you back onto the road. Note the character of this L-shaped old stable block, with an old mullioned window but a very modern roof.

Bear left along the road for Hampsthwaite, re-crossing Bracken Bridge but varying the entry into the village just after the church tower appears ahead. Reaching a bend at the village sign, bear left along a gem of a part-flagged, leafy byway (a medieval way possibly upon a Roman route) to emerge into the churchyard. The church of St Thomas a'Becket was much restored by the Victorians, but the tower is a good 500 years old. A path runs along the front of the church and out onto the village street, with the centre just to the right along Church Lane.

Hampsthwaite church

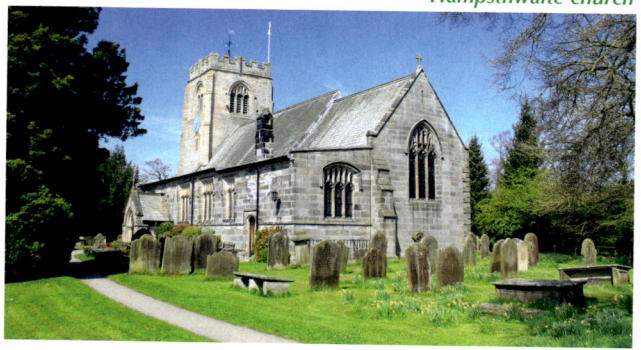

17 NIDD VALLEY

4 miles from Birstwith

The banks of the Nidd lead to a stunning old bridge before open rambling over the fields

Start Village centre (SE 244597; HG3 2NF), roadside parking
Map OS Explorer 298, Nidderdale

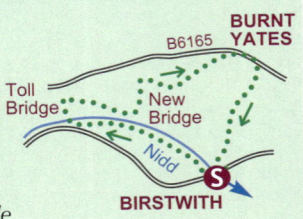

Dominated by a feeds mill, Birstwith is a colourful village with a Post office/shop, the Station Hotel, and the elegant spired St James' church. From the vicinity of the pub, head south on the street to cross the bridge on the Nidd. A little further turn right, upstream with a mill-cut by sports fields. This runs to a weir to trace the river upstream. The path soon takes a straight hedgeside course, rejoining the river for a super stroll to an old track just short of the graceful arch of New Bridge. Dating from around 1615, it was rebuilt in 1822. From a stile on its near side resume upstream through two riverside fields to a stile onto the valley road. Don't join it but turn right on a private toll road, crossing Ross Bridge to a red-brick cottage at the old railway.

A minute further, leave by a stile on the right and follow a stream to the old rail embankment. An unofficial but popular short alternative path joins the line at a stile on it, and runs left along the wooded embankment to meet the main route at an enclosed old way leading from New Bridge. The main route uses a ladder-stile ahead to shadow the embankment to where a bridle-gate takes you over the old line to a stile. In the slim pasture behind go left between railway and river, broadening at a bridle-gate to lead back to a stile at New Bridge.

Leave the river by going left along the enclosed old way embowered in greenery, soon re-crossing the old line and rising delightfully between walls. Emerging at the top into a field, the now sunken way rises left up the side, soon re-establishing its old guise at a gate above. A second grand section takes you further uphill: just after a stile on the left it levels out, here leave by a stile on the right. Cross a field to a gate onto a drive at Dinmore House. Turn right into the grounds and on between houses. In the yard cross to a gate ahead, across a garden to another gate. A grassy path runs into trees to quickly reach a gate into a small rough enclosure. Ignore the gate ahead and rise left to a barn conversion. Through a gate on the right in front of it, gently ascend with the left-hand wall up three fields: a final stile puts you onto the B6165 at Burnt Yates.

Turn right on the footway into the centre, and leave by a rough access road past the former Bay Horse pub immediately after St Andrew's church. This winds round past housing to approach Church Farm at the end. Here take a track left to a gate/stile into a field. Follow the grassy track down through a gate to fade at an old gateway on a bend. Here bear right with an old hedge to meet a wall, going left with it to a kissing-gate. Descending the fieldside, transfer to the other side of the fence at a stile in a tiny wall. Resume to a gate at the bottom, then bear right down to a corner gate onto a drive at West House. Turn down this onto suburban Nidd Lane, left to Station Road on the village edge, and right to finish.

New Bridge above Birstwith

18 BRAISTY WOODS

4¾ miles from Dacre Banks

Lovely woodland and riverside scenery either side of Low Laithe

Start Village centre (SE 196619; HG3 4AN), car park by pub
Map OS Explorer 298, Nidderdale

Dacre Banks is a pleasant village with the Royal Oak pub and a shop. From the green take the short lane past the pub, quickly branching left down into a yard. Drop down and along to the right near more houses, and at the end take a gate on the left by an outhouse. Follow the wallside to a gate from where a thin path crosses to the river. Turn left to trace the Nidd upstream past sports grounds to a road bridge. Cross to the former timber yard, and slightly left an enclosed path is ushered round the perimeter. At the far end the river is rejoined at a weir. Ignore a kissing-gate in the fence for a path upstream. Faced with a wooded bank at the end, use a kissing-gate and another just beyond to join a rough road. Turn right, crossing the old railway, and remain on the road parallel with the railway, keeping right at a fork as it opens out.

Passing a lone house and a timber yard a continuing track runs to a gate at the end. Advance on the hedgeside, and through a corner gate a firmer track comes in to run to Harewell Hall Farm. The old house with its mullioned windows is well seen just below: high above is the Brimham Rocks skyline across the dale. Drop right into the yard behind the main house. Opposite the door take a gate on the left and a grassy track slants down to the old railway, over which cross to a footbridge on the tree-lined river.

Cross and turn downstream, this delightful stretch ends when deflected left with inflowing Fell Beck. This is shortly crossed by a footbridge, and just upstream the path rises up a field onto the road in Low Laithe. Turn right on the footway into this small settlement. Past Ye Olde Oak Inn cross the road, and by the bus shelter turn up a short driveway. A path continues up the side of a wood, by abundant hollies past a recolonised quarry. At the top leave by a corner stile, just above which turn left on a track towards Braisty Woods. It passes through a gate and a belt of trees to a junction in the hamlet, where turn right on the access road. A big mullioned windowed house stands on the left. Advance on past all the buildings and a pond, and as the road swings left, keep straight on an access road leading to Owenwell House. A charming grassy cart track continues along the base of the woods to end at isolated Woolwich Farm.

Keep on a brief flagged section between a couple of gates and past a fine old barn to a ramshackle barn at a wood corner. The left-hand gate puts you into the trees, and a super path runs on the wood edge. Beyond a wall-stile it enters Old Spring Wood, an ancient wood with hollies in profusion. Initially bearing slightly right, it runs on to emerge beneath a lone house and above a big pond. Keep on to join its short drive out onto the road at Hartwith Bank. Turn down to the main road in Summerbridge. Here are the Flying Dutchman pub, a Post office, shops and tearoom. Cross straight over and down Dawson Bank to cross the bridge on the Nidd, remaining on the road past the church into Dacre Banks.

At Braisty Woods

19 BRIMHAM MOOR

4¾ miles from Brimham Rocks

Easy walking through a colourful landscape

Start National Trust car park
(SE 208645; HG3 4DW)
Map OS Explorer 298, Nidderdale

Brimham Rocks form an extensive collection of millstone grit outcrops, sculpted into wonderfully bizarre shapes by millennia of Yorkshire weather. From the car park return to the road crossing Brimham Moor, and 100 yards to the right, turn off left on a broad, inviting path through rolling heather. Further back, some of the celebrated rocks rise from bracken and woodland surrounds. At the end a stile by a gate in a boundary wall sees you off the moor, and a nice path heads away through still colourful terrain. This emerges onto a farm drive beneath Riva Hill, and runs to a corner. Here leave the farm road which swings left, and take a gate to the right, where a green track heads away. This runs a lengthy enclosed way as a cart track to ultimately emerge onto a road.

Ignoring the road take a farm road left to Brimham Lodge. Savour the remarkable facade of this lovely house, dating from the 1660s and boasting an astonishing array of mullioned windows. Outside its garden wall a mounting block supports a stone shaft sporting an old sundial. Remain on the access road left of the house, through the yard and down the slope beyond (ignoring a left branch). This same track continues along a wood edge and on to Park House. Pass right of the buildings along another walled green track. At the end the track swings right along a wallside to a gateway at the end, where it swings left above wildfowl ponds. Remain on this to Beck Side Farm, and out on its drive. Crossing a streamlet, fork left off the drive up an enclosed green way by a garden and out onto a narrow lane alongside an old chapel.

Turn left into trees and across a streamlet. As it rises away, take a cart track right along the edge of the trees. It drops to cross a streamlet and rises gently to a gate out of the wood. Keep straight on with a line of trees to Summer Wood House. Through the yard head up the drive onto Brimham Moor, rising to meet the road. Cross to a little path rising to large outcrops above. Behind, a thin path rises right to quickly meet a level path. Go left, running just 50 yards above those outcrops, a grand course across the moor with slightly higher ground on your right. Dropping gently and soon reaching a fork, ignore the main one dropping to a lay-by, and bear right on the lesser, level one. Undulating along, in front of a knoll it merges with a broader one from an even closer lay-by.

Forge on over a rocky-floored knoll, and reaching a fork, take the left one onto a rock platform. Slip down to the right and along the base of a tall rockface. Go right 50 yards to a very broad path with an iconic shapely boulder to the left, and advance to join an even broader path just beyond. Go right, quickly joining a surfaced access road. The visitor centre/shop is just around to the right, based in Brimham House dating from 1792. Note that a path just beyond it offers a nice detour to further outstanding formations. From this junction by the café/WC, a tarmac path swings back left beneath the distinctive Eagle boulders. Quickly forking, keep to the right one to run through the heart of this fascinating area, and all too soon you will arrive back at the car park.

At Brimham Rocks

20 PANORAMA WALK

3 miles from Pateley Bridge

A simple ramble with suitably big views and a riverside return

Start Town centre (SE 157655; HG3 5JU), car parks
Map OS Explorer 298, Nidderdale

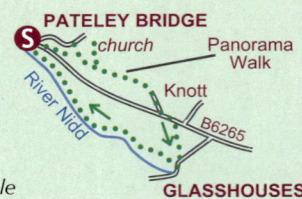

For a note on Pateley Bridge, see page 48. From the bridge at the foot of High Street head east up the main thoroughfare, swinging right at the top. As the road levels out after the Methodist church, a footpath sign points up a flight of steps to the start of the Panorama Walk. A steep, enclosed path climbs past an inscribed stone tablet above a well. Immediately beyond the cemetery entrance turn left onto a walled path offering views over Gouthwaite Reservoir beyond the gravestones. It runs along to the old church of St Mary the Virgin hidden in trees. Dating from the 14th century, it was abandoned in 1826 due to poor access, insufficient size and repair costs, being replaced by St Cuthbert's in the town.

Resume by following the path up the churchyard a few paces to a wooden kissing-gate in the wall on the right. Cross the field to a gate, and on again to a stile at the end. A few enclosed strides put you back onto the Panorama Walk. The easing gradient of this narrow surfaced way quickly leads to an iron gate accessing a viewing platform on a craggy knoll, the Victorians' Pulpit Rock. A magnificent prospect of Guise Cliff across the valley features the two surviving towers of Yorke's Folly. Continuing, the gradient eases further and levels out to reach the exclusive hamlet of Knott, its houses set back from open greens. Keep straight on its surfaced access road which bears right to drop down to the main road.

Two minutes along the footway to the left, cross to a kissing-gate just past the last house. A flagged path descends a fieldside to another kissing-gate, from where an enclosed path drops onto a rough lane on the edge of Glasshouses. Turn left on this access road to emerge onto the sloping green of this village dominated by its tall church spire. The village's existence owes much to the Metcalfe family, who erected housing and public buildings in the mid-19th century for workers in their large flax-spinning mill.

Turn right on the road along the bottom edge of the green, descending past the former railway station and the school to approach Glasshouses Bridge alongside Glasshouses Mill of 1874. Boasting an imposing facade with an old clock and large bell, this substantial old mill enjoys an impressive riverside frontage and is now being transformed into residential use with cafe and shop. Without crossing the bridge take the broad carriageway upstream for an infallible and dead-flat return to Pateley Bridge. At once the drive is sandwiched between a large millpond and a mill-cut.

The river is regained at a weir marking the start of the mill-cut. Across it is the gaunt mansion of Castlestead, erected in 1862 for the mill-owning Metcalfes. The Nidd is now traced upstream on a broad pathway offering a lovely riverbank stroll: the course of the railway is evident during the final stages. The former Nidd Valley Railway opened in 1862 by the North Eastern Railway was a typical rural branch line from near Harrogate to its terminus at Pateley Bridge. The single-track line finally succumbed in 1964, having been closed to passengers 13 years earlier. Path and river run together to re-enter town.

The old church above Pateley Bridge

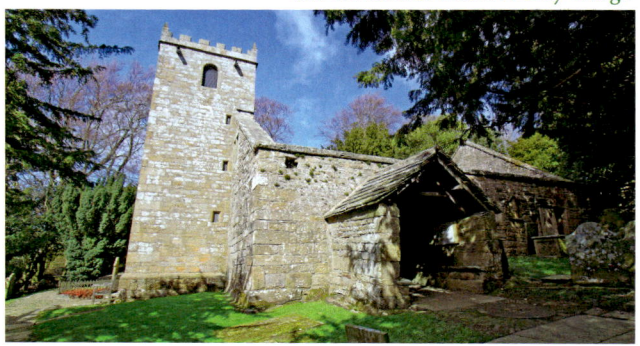

21   TRAMWAY TO WATH

4 miles from Pateley Bridge

Absorbing rambling by old tramway and old railway, with an old village and stunning views

Start Town centre (SE 157655; HG3 5JU), car parks
Map OS Explorer 298, Nidderdale

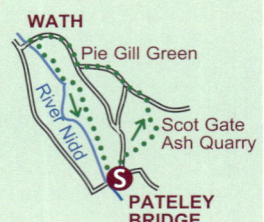

For a note on Pateley Bridge, see page 48. From the bridge head up High Street and turn left on Church Street. Past the church of St Cuthbert continue opposite the museum in the old workhouse, then rising to become Wath Road. After the last row of houses on the left it bridges the course of a tramway that served Scot Gate Ash Quarry high above. A wall-stile gives access to the grassy incline whose steep course leads unfailingly to the old workings. The upper stage becomes open and steeper alongside a wood, and from a stile at the top, only a minute's more climbing awaits. This extensive site produced delphstone, a strong millstone grit used in platforms and public buildings. The tramway was operated by steel ropes, with loaded trucks descending a maximum 1 in 3 gradient as they assisted empty ones return to the top. The descent of 600 feet over a distance of 1000 yards ended at a railway yard.

With a house to your right advance a few steps to the ruinous winding house. Here bear left on a grassy path, rapidly merging with another as it runs left between spoil heaps. This super path soon joins a fence/wall on the left to skirt the boundary of the quarry's heathery environs, giving big views across the valley. Emergence at the far end is a stunning moment as views up to the dalehead feature Great Whernside and Little Whernside beyond Gouthwaite Reservoir. Head on through a gate in a wall ahead to cross to another onto Wath Lane. This quiet byway leads all the way back to the valley, an extended descent in which you can concentrate on the panorama dominated by the reservoir.

At a junction continue ahead, down to another junction at Pie Gill Green. Turn right for a couple of minutes into Wath. This tiny, unspoiled settlement boasts a fine wooded setting with much of interest. First is the tiny Methodist chapel of 1859 affixed to a cottage. At the bend beyond is an old mill with bell, weathervane and workers' cottages. The Sportsmans Arms has a fine individual sign, while across from it is the old station house. Remain on the road as it turns sharp left past the hotel, over the old railway and along to Wath Bridge. Though widened in 1890 it is small enough to recall the days when it served the monks of Fountains Abbey.

Without crossing the bridge take a footbridge on the left: a path crosses a field centre to a wall-stile, continuing on to meet the gently embanked course of the railway. From the next kissing-gate the line is followed for some distance to a point where the Nidd comes in alongside. A stile admits to this tree-shrouded setting, and the railway is then forsaken for the river as a kissing-gate puts you onto its tree-lined bank. This leads unerringly back to Pateley Bridge. Ignoring a modern footbridge on the river, keep on a firmer path to soon reach a weir. Here the path becomes confined alongside new housing, and is deflected away to emerge between buildings onto Mill Lane adjacent to Pateley's graceful bridge.

Gouthwaite Reservoir from above Wath

22 FOSTER BECK WATERMILL

4 miles from Pateley Bridge

Riverbank walking to a remarkable waterwheel and sweeping views on a gentle upland return

Start Town centre
(SE 157655; HG3 5JU), car parks
Map OS Explorer 298, Nidderdale

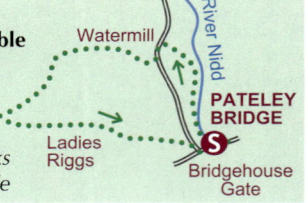

Pateley Bridge is undisputed capital of Nidderdale: to locals it is the hub of dale life, to visitors, the first stop. Within this compact little town (a village in size) are pubs, cafes, information centre, and individual and absorbing shops hidden down inviting alleys. The Nidderdale Museum carries absorbing displays of local life gone by, including Pateley Bridge's abandoned industries of lead mining, quarrying and railways. Pateley is also home to the colourful and hugely popular Nidderdale Show each September.

From the foot of High Street, cross the bridge and turn right into the public park. Remaining on the tree-lined riverbank, the embanked, initially surfaced path leads past a caravan site before gaining open fields alongside a footbridge on the river. In the second field the path cuts the corner at Foster Beck's entry into the Nidd, to a kissing-gate to the right of Brigg House Farm. Alongside a cottage a footbridge crosses the beck, now followed upstream to another kissing-gate before crossing to one onto a road junction at Corn Close. Turn left, briefly, along the road to the Bridge Inn which replaced the neighbouring Watermill Inn. The original pub occupied the flax mill that was a ropemakers into the 1960s, and restoration of the waterwheel in 1990 made it an attraction in its own right. With the building transformed into apartments, the 35-foot diameter wheel is well seen from the car park.

Continue a little further along the road to a sharp bend, and turn along a stony drive to Mosscarr Farm (a bungalow), ignoring an uphill fork en route as the track opens out to run more pleasantly. Continuing behind converted barns clustered island-like in the field-centre, the track runs on to a gate into an idyllically sited cottage at Mosscarr Bottom. Out through another gate, ignore a footbridge and ford in a wooded dell, and take a kissing-gate to the left. Here a superb grassy way rises left with the wall through colourful country with unfolding views. At the top corner it passes through a gate and rises to join a firmer track. Just 30 yards further however, with a gate in sight ahead, the invisible right of way bears right, crossing the pasture to find a kissing-gate in the fence ahead, here joining a surfaced access road.

Turn left on this narrow lane rising onto Ladies Riggs, a lofty brow with outstanding views both up-dale and down-dale. A few minutes beyond Riggs House Farm the road enters a shroud of trees: here leave it through the few trees on the left to a stile in a corner. A grand stride follows the hedge downhill with Pateley Bridge ahead. Keeping field boundaries on the right, at a kissing-gate the way becomes enclosed to run a super hedgerowed course down onto an access driveway at a lone house. Continue down this onto a back road at Bridgehouse Gate. Just in front is the former Metcalf's Brewery, which retains its typical brewhouse appearance. Go right to the main road by the Royal Oak, then left back over the bridge into town.

Foster Beck Watermill

23 GUISE CLIFF

4 miles from Bewerley

A stunning range of scenery from woodland to moorland, and a classic Nidderdale landmark

Start *Village centre (SE 156649; HG3 5HX), roadside parking*
Map *OS Explorer 298, Nidderdale*

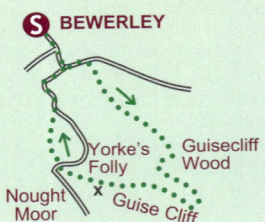

Bewerley is an attractive village with cottages set back from a green. Head south on the footway through the village, passing Bewerley Grange Chapel, a grange of Fountains Abbey. Drop past a junction to a T-junction across Turner Bridge, and go a short way left as far as a bridle-gate on the right. A grassy way runs between paddocks and through a gate at the end. This faint way runs on two fieldsides to a gate. Resume on the other side of the hedge, through a gate alongside a house where a grassy track forms to reach a gate at Baylis Gap Farm. Go forward the short way onto a firm track. With the farm to the left keep on the track rising away, a local alternative to the invisible path up the adjacent field. When the track emerges into a field at the top and turns sharp right, keep on a thin wallside path to a gate/stile at the end into Guisecliff Wood.

A good path rises away through boulder-strewn woodland. A brief fork at a hollow is irrelevant as they merge just beyond, then merge into a broader path rising from the left. The steady rise soon swings sharply right uphill, climbing more steeply to briefly level out. Here it forks, the onward route slanting up to the left. Firstly, a 100-yard detour rises right to boulders on the shore of Guisecliff Tarn, an unexpected gem. The main path winds steeply up again before levelling out between boulders. A brief descent soon levels out for a delightful section that runs for some time to ultimately leave the trees. Ignoring a gate just ahead, a good path slants right through bracken to a wall: turn to ascend with it, the bracken ending just before the final rise to the corner by a mast.

Through a gate onto Heyshaw Moor cross the access track and advance only to its fence corner, then leave the broad path for a thinner one going right to cut back to the wall heading away. After an immediate stile in a fence, a minute further the wall ends at the exposed beginnings of Guise Cliff. This harbours crevices around which dogs and children should be on a tight rein. Beyond the imposing rock architecture overlooking the woodland blanket below is a wonderful panorama, with Gouthwaite Reservoir up-dale. With a fence to the left, the path runs left on the crest.

As the edge abates the wall returns and the path runs to a stile where the parallel fence joins the wall. The wallside path continues on the moor edge to the waiting towers of Yorke's Folly, gained by a bridle-gate in the wall. This landmark was built 200 years ago, and one of three original towers succumbed to a storm in 1893. Beyond, the path descends through heather to a parking area on Nought Bank. From the kissing-gate behind, a path descends the heathery moor to a kissing-gate in a wall. It then winds down into the top of Skrikes Wood, slanting right down to a kissing-gate out of the trees. A faint grassy way slants down a large field to a kissing-gate back onto Nought Bank Road. Go left and along to the junction at Turner Bridge, retracing steps to finish.

Looking up Nidderdale from Guise Cliff

24 GREENHOW MINES

3¾ miles from Greenhow

Intriguing lead mining remains explored from largely firm tracks

Start Toft Gate (Coldstones Cut), a mile east of village on B6265 (SE 129643; HG3 5AE), car park
Map OS Explorer 298, Nidderdale

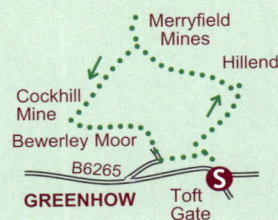

A novel feature of this walk is that its highest point is the start. Greenhow is a remote former lead mining community, and until its closure the Miners Arms was one of England's highest pubs. Toft Gate is base for an industrial heritage trail, explored by a path accessing the remains of a square chimney at the top of the flue. A continuation path then runs down to the principal feature, a massive vertical kiln dating from the 1860s. Also just a few minutes' uphill walk from here is Coldstones Cut, an impressive stone 'art' construction overlooking the modern day quarry.

Start by crossing the main road to a stile at the left-hand gate opposite, immediately enjoying extensive views to moors above Upper Nidderdale. A faint grassy way slants down to a gate then down again, left of a barn to trace the wall to a corner stile. A trod runs to a bridle-gate onto an access road just ahead. Turn right to houses at Coldstonesfold, continuing down a grassy track that becomes a sunken way above a plantation. Reaching a gate by a streamlet, it runs along to join a drive beneath Ivin Waite. Turn down its enclosed course to a junction with a surfaced access road. Double back left on this to its imminent split at Low Hole Bottom. Bear right, rising past the house at Hillend then opening out in more colourful surrounds to reach Brandstone Dub Bridge.

Across, the stony track climbs steeply outside a wood, levelling out to be joined by one from the right. Keep on the moorland flank of Nabs to a junction. The walk resumes here after a detour to look down on Merryfield mining site. Advance straight on a nicer track to a gateway, and a little further along you reach a good vantage point above spoil heaps overlooking the mines. The Prosperous Smelt Mill is a large ruinous building by the beck, with a geared winding shaft, a peat store and a prominent old flue.

For the onward route return to the junction and pass through the gate/stile on the main track. Ignoring a right fork, remain on this walled way as it rises away. At a T-junction above an isolated house turn right, up to bend left to a gate accessing the valley of Brandstone Beck again. The track gently declines into the gill and the environs of Cockhill Lead Mine, passing an arch of Providence smelt mill. The track fords the beck and rises to a junction at the mine site. A mine level is sited directly under the track here. The track now cuts back sharply left, rising gently away. Looking back, a smelt mill chimney appears on the moor above the workings. The way crosses to a wall corner then ascends steeply to a gate/stile off the moor. A walled road climbs away, absorbing a farm drive before easing out. At a sharp right bend just ahead, take a gate on the left onto the Coldstonesfold road heading away. As it turns to drop more firmly left, a stile on the right sends a grassy path along the wallside, rising further on to arrive back at the outward path by a gate. Re-ascend the field back to the road above.

At Providence Smelt Mill

25 — HOW STEAN GORGE

3¼ miles from Lofthouse

Old villages amid magical natural attractions in Upper Nidderdale

Start Village centre (SE 101734; HG3 5SA), car park
Map OS Explorer 298, Nidderdale *or* OL30, Yorkshire Dales North/Central

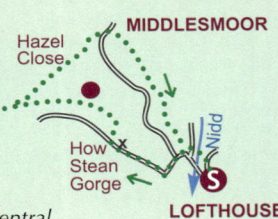

For a note on Lofthouse see page 56. From the fountain take a gap in the left corner of the square between cottages, and after a few yards of track a bridle-gate sends a path down to a footbridge on the Nidd. Cross to emerge onto a road, straight over to a kissing-gate and past a cricket pitch onto another road. Go briefly right then fork left. Past a car park keep right as the road runs to How Stean Gorge. If opting to explore the gorge, pay entrance fees at the cafe/gift shop. How Stean Gorge is a limestone ravine half a mile long and up to 80 feet deep, its rocks worn into dramatic contours by the action of water: deep, dark and wet caves abound.

Resume across the bridge to the car park field and take a gate at the top left corner. Advance to a gate by a barn, then go left across several field-centres, using gates in walls beneath Hazel Close Farm to a path junction at a wall-stile. Through it a path slants down to a bridle-gate above the beck, with a footbridge just below. Don't pass through, but turn upstream to a wall-stile then a kissing-gate, from where a little path drops gently to the beck. On by a low limestone scar, at the end ignore a gate in front, and instead use a nick in the scar to resume to a kissing-gate into a wooded bank by the beck. Through bracken and scattered trees, the path later slants up the wooded bank to a brow.

While the route doubles back here from a kissing-gate just above, first consider a detour to How Stean Force. Advance over a streamlet then drop down to a gate into a large pasture. Advance outside a wood corner to a path junction just short of a stone-arched bridge. From a bridle-gate into trees on the left, a path runs the few yards to a viewpoint for the falls. Now retrace steps to the kissing-gate on the brow. From it a grassy path climbs very briefly through bracken, then bears right to cross to a stile at the foot of a wall. Follow a fence away to another wall-stile, then cross a field up to a gateway. From a gate in the top corner a path descends a wooded enclosure onto the road at the entrance to Middlesmoor, opposite an old chapel. The name of Nidderdale's first village aptly describes its position, on a broad tongue between the two valleys. Just above you, the Crown pub occupies an attractive corner.

    Leave by making for St Chad's church by a cobbled street after the phonebox. Containing a Saxon cross, it is best known for its churchyard foreground to a view down the dale to Gouthwaite Reservoir. To its right a squeezer-stile sees a short snicket down to a gate. A flight of steps drops into a field, and a path maintains a straight line to Halfway House Farm. Go straight through the yard to a gate at the bottom, and head down the right side of a field to a stile. At the bottom swing left to a stile part way along, then bear left to a corner stile into the lay-by near the start. Retrace steps over the footbridge, but first consider a five-minute detour upstream for the shy charms of Nidd Falls.

How Stean Gorge

26 THROPE EDGE

3 miles from Lofthouse

A steep climb earns outstanding views over Upper Nidderdale

Start *Village centre (SE 101734; HG3 5SA), car park*
Map *OS Explorer 298, Nidderdale* **or** *OL30, Yorkshire Dales North/Central*

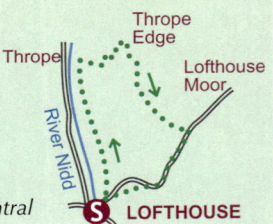

Lofthouse is a tidy village high above the river, featuring the Crown Hotel and an attractive corner with a fountain which bears absorbing words. Alongside the school and WC on the bottom road is the old station house, highest on the old Nidd Valley Light Railway. Leave by the Masham road passing the Peace Memorial before climbing away from the houses. Farmhouse ice cream may be available on the left. Before the first bend take a grassy track running left. This is Thrope Lane, and beyond a gate it leads an unerring, mile-long course to Thrope Farm. Early on, ignore a right branch to a gate ahead, keeping to the level one. Already you have good views across to Middlesmoor from this splendid old track. There is a brief glimpse of your objective of the shooting house on Thrope Edge, appearing as a church silhouetted on the skyline. The track becomes enclosed for the final section to the farm.

As you draw level with the farm take a gate on the right to negotiate sheep pens, past a barn and up the wallside. Towards the top bear left to a gate in the fence above. Entering more colourful surrounds rise left with the fence, an old green way soon forking. Ignoring its sunken continuation, instead bear right up a similarly good track. This ascends a steep, sunken course through scattered silver birch and bracken, then swings left to rise more steadily above the trees and beneath scattered rocks. Outstanding views open out over the upper dale. This finely engineered old way slants all the way up to a gate in the wall above, and through it the shooting house is revealed a little higher. Two thinner paths initially depart, but both bear left to quickly merge amid bracken. The path rises a short way further before branching left to resume its engineered course, visible ahead as it slants left to gain the skyline of Thrope Edge just left of the house. This is emphatically the place to halt and embrace the big views along the length of the dale. A fine contrast is formed by the lush green of the valley at your feet and the dark outlines of rounded Meugher, Great Whernside and Little Whernside on the western skyline, with Menwith Hill and Greenhow Hill way down the valley.

Turn right on the broad shooters' track alongside, enjoying only a short spell above the edge before a wall deflects the track left. Within a minute take a gate in the wall and a grassier track heads away across the moor, joined by a wall on the left. Immediately after passing above a recolonised quarry, the track forks into thinner trods. Bear left to a gate in the nearby wall, where Gouthwaite Reservoir makes its big appearance ahead. The gentle track steadily declines through two moorland enclosures to a gate onto Pott Moor High Road. Turn right to commence a steep descent back to Lofthouse, with views featuring Gouthwaite, the Stean Valley and Middlesmoor. When the road breaks free turn down the wallside for a more direct, grassy descent to the edge of the village.

The shooting house on Thrope Edge

27   SCAR HOUSE RESERVOIR

4 miles from Scar House

A simple circuit of this windswept reservoir in its bleak upland setting

Start Yorkshire Water car park at private road end, reached from near Lofthouse (SE 069766; HG3 5SW)
Map OS Explorer OL30, Yorkshire Dales North/Central

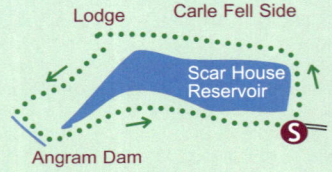

    Alongside the car park is a bunkhouse and WC, with occasional refreshments, while information panels abound. From the car park join the water company road which runs past the dam of Scar House Reservoir, not crossed until the end of the walk. Both this and Angram Reservoir were the handiwork of Bradford Corporation to slake the thirsts of its rapidly growing population, each boasting a masonry dam of which Scar House's rises to a height of some 150 feet. The road runs above the entire length of the southern shore, rising very slightly as it goes. At the dalehead, the rippling shoulders of Great Whernside form a comprehensive barrier: over to the right is flat-topped Little Whernside.

    The road eventually gains the foot of Angram Reservoir, not seen until you are almost there. Just short of it, a rest house offers useful shelter. Identical in character (though Scar House is double the size) Angram was completed in 1913, 23 years before its lower neighbour. Cross the dam to its northern end, and while the road turns left and expires, your way is immediately right onto an excellent green path, running gently downstream and soon swinging left to begin a contour that is joined by a wall and interrupted only by the slight dip of Wench Gill. Good views look down over Scar House Reservoir to Carle Fell and Dale Edge. Rising back out to a gate/stile soon followed by another, the path is soon rejoined by a wall. Just beyond a gate in a solid wall you reach a corner gate at the start of an enclosed green way.

An option here is to immediately join the waterside path, in which case pass through a gate/stile on the right and descend the wallside to the shore. Go left through a gate to another rest house, then simply trace an excellent path all the way back to the end of the dam. The higher route turns left up the grassy, walled track which quickly swings right to a junction with a firmer track. Turn right here to immediately reach Lodge. Low level ruins survive from what was originally a medieval hunting lodge, and a working farm until a century ago. Embowered in trees, this location is prominent in all views around this dalehead. The last ruin on the right was a Methodist chapel.

The track leads out through a gate back into open slopes above Scar House Reservoir's northern shore. You could opt to join the shoreline path by dropping down the rough pasture: either way, enjoy big views beyond the dam to the magnificent sweep of the upper valley beneath the moors of Dale Edge. Across the valley below the car park is the site of a village that existed during the construction years: this complete settlement had a population of over 1000 in the 1920s. On the hillsides, meanwhile, are quarries opened to win stone for the dams. The track passes close by the old reservoir keeper's house to reach the dam. Finally cross it to return to the car park.

Scar House Reservoir

28 EAVESTONE LAKE

4¼ miles from Sawley

Pleasant rural rambling to a lovely wooded lake

Start *Village centre (SE 248677; HG4 3EE), roadside parking*
Map *OS Explorer 298, Nidderdale*

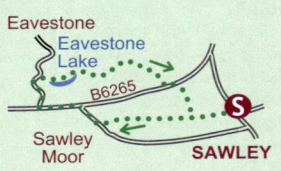

Sawley is a small village in estate country near Fountains Abbey. Its tiny church stands across from the Sawley Arms, while an old schoolhouse at the top of the green is now the village hall. From the green follow the access road briefly up its left side, then with the Parish Room and a drive on your left, take a wall-stile to rise right up the hedgeside. Up a second field you reach a short hedgerowed path running right out into another field. Resume left up to the top corner, through which is a cross-paths at the end of a rough enclosed lane. Over the stile pass through a gate/stile on your right and resume your upward line with a fence on your left. This straight course is maintained through a number of fields, levelling out and on through a series of stiles to the far end where a short enclosed path by a shed puts you onto Sawley Moor Lane.

Turn right alongside woodland, passing through Picking Gill nature reserve amid old quarries. Emerging onto the dead-straight B6265 Pateley Bridge-Ripon road, turn left for ten minutes then escape right down the Eavestone cul-de-sac. Bear right down past the farm. As the road swings sharp left, drop a little then take a path doubling back into the wood. Here begins a glorious spell on a good path in magnificent surroundings. First feature is the upper reservoir of Eavestone Lake, with a large crag jutting into the water. The gritstone surrounding these two lakes yields numerous rock climbs on at least sixteen separate buttresses. Across its outflow the path winds round to the head of Eavestone Lake, then runs its full length, a half-hour of sheer delight. Of immediate interest are the outcrops of Ravens Crag above the opposite bank.

Rising slightly from the shore part way on, the path quickly drops back to it, passing an old boathouse to reach a fork at the end. Bear right to cross a small dam and a little arched bridge. Joining a rough track, cross straight over as your path makes a sustained pull through Fishpond Wood. From a stile at the top bear left across the field to a stile onto the drive to Hollin Hill Farm. Go left around to the new house, and straight on through a scrubby corner to its left. Big views over a rolling landscape include the tower of Fountains Abbey. A thin path drops the short way to a stile into a field corner. Bear briefly right to locate a stile into a slim enclosure. Go left along it, and as it opens out keep with its right side to run to a gate into West Gowbusk at the end.

Go straight through the farmyard and out on the drive, but immediately leave by a bridle-gate on the left. This accesses a gate to the front of a cottage at Gowbusk, to follow its drive back out onto the B6265. Go briefly left to a stile on the right. Cross the field to a stile in the far corner, then rise gently along the fieldsides. Broad views look across to the distant North York Moors: note also the spire of Studley Royal church. Reaching the rough enclosed lane again, take the stile on your left to retrace opening steps down into the village.

Eavestone Lake

29   STUDLEY ROYAL

4½ miles from Fountains Abbey

Elegant walking through a deer park and delightful valley

Start National Trust Visitor Centre (SE 272686; HG4 3DY), car park
Map OS Explorer 298, Nidderdale **or** 299, Ripon & Boroughbridge

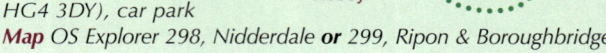

Fountains Abbey and Studley Royal is a World Heritage Site, with a combination of beautiful ruins and water gardens. Founded in 1132, the abbey forms the most extensive Cistercian remains in England, and its setting in the wooded valley of the River Skell is unsurpassed: the adjacent water gardens with various follies were laid out in the 18th century. While this walk visits Studley Royal deer park, it is worth making a day of it to savour the 'paying' attractions. By the roundabout at the visitor centre, a bridleway runs through trees parallel with the access road to your left. This emerges by the road at a pedestrian entrance to Studley Park, with a tall obelisk of 1815 dwarfed by the spire of St Mary's church. Through the gate, pass the obelisk and advance to the church, completed in 1878 and open afternoons from Easter to September.

You are now within the deer park, and are quite likely to encounter some or all of a range of Red, Fallow and Sika deer. From opposite the church gate a grassy path descends to the car park above the abbey's east entrance by the lake. Here is a shop, tearoom, WCs and ticket office for entry to the abbey and water gardens. Follow the drive left alongside the lake, and at the end bear right to a wooden bridge over the outflow. Here begins the walk through the Valley of Seven Bridges in tandem with the River Skell. This is accompanied downstream through the encroaching walls of this steep-sided valley, a delightful amble re-crossing the river on five further occasions, each by means of identical stone-arched bridges. The river disappears underground part way along.

After the last one the estate is vacated at a tall gate, and a woodland path runs down to the seventh bridge.

Leave the broadening track and cross the plain bridge, joining a broader way from the left to ascend a wooded hollow to a track junction at the top. Turn right on a broad pathway, soon reaching the wood edge to begin a long, imperceptible rise inside the wall enclosing the wood. Reaching the ruin of Mackershaw Lodge, leave the path for a gate in the old archway, re-entering the park. A broad grassy path heads away, passing a small pond on the right and then sweeping down on a grassy cart track, with a larger pond to your left. Leaving the park at a tall gate, it descends a wooded bank to arrive back at the lake outflow.

Re-cross and follow the track away to rejoin the access road. Go right to rise briefly to a crossroads with the main driveway. Up to your left is the church, framed beyond an avenue of limes. Cross straight over on the hard road opposite, running a grand, level course through the open park to a junction with an access road to the Studley Royal former stable block of 1732 to your left. At this exact point double back sharp left on a delectable grassy path. This runs a level course to meet the driveway rising right the short way to the church, passing the Choristers' House. Now simply retrace steps to the visitor centre.

The Lake at Studley Royal

30 THE URE AT RIPON

3³⁄4 miles from Ripon

Riverbank walking on the edge of an absorbing tiny city

Start North Bridge (SE 316720; HG4 1HX), roadside parking
Map OS Explorer 299, Ripon & Boroughbridge

Where Magdalen's Road meets the main road turn right over North Bridge on the Ure. Across, bear right towards a roundabout, but before it keep right with the river under the by-pass. On the other side a path clings to the river alongside a road: when it turns off at a red-brick hut join it, following its footway gently up to 13th century Sharow Cross. This is the last survivor of eight that gave sanctuary to fugitives within a mile of the city. Bear right here on narrower Sharow Lane, along the village edge to drop down to a grassy triangle. Just a little further along is the Half Moon Inn.

Turn right on a long, hedgerowed track which later becomes grassier then narrower to emerge into a field alongside a wood. A path continues, and beyond the wood end take a bridle-gate in the adjacent hedge. Strike across the arable field centre to join an embanked riverbank path. While your onward route is right, a brief diversion left to Hewick Bridge reveals the concrete remains of a ford used by tanks during Second World War training.

Turning upstream, the path runs an uncomplicated course by the Ure, initially through scrub, but then largely on the wooded bank. Whilst a path runs unfailingly back to the start, erosion has seen the right of way deflected from the bank near the end: this comes at a kissing-gate on the right, from where a path bears right across the field-end to ascend a short, steep bank into trees at Bell Banks. Running left through a kissing-gate back into woodland, it runs a level course above the steep wooded drop to the river. Before long the path descends back to the bank. Resume with the river to soon pick up the outward route.